WINTER SEX

WINTER SEX

Poems by

Katy Lederer

Verse Press
Amherst, MA

Published by Verse Press

Library of Congress Cataloging-in-Publication Data
Lederer, Katy.
　　Winter sex : poems / by Katy Lederer.
　　　　p. cm.
　　ISBN 0-9703672-8-7 (pbk.)
　　I. Title.
　　PS3612.E3417 W56 2002
　　811'.6—dc21

　　　　　　　　　　　　2002001738

Printed in the United States of America

9 8 7 6 5 4 3 2 1
FIRST EDITION

ACKNOWLEDGMENTS: *American Poetry Review*: "A Dream of Mimesis," "In Las Vegas," "A New Way to Live," "An Interrupted Question." *Arshile*: "In Brooklyn." *Cello Entry*: "Sick and Sin," "The Wages of Sin." *East Village Poetry Web*: "Immaculation," "False Life." *Fence*: "Pursuant." *Gare du Nord*: "According to the Appetites." *Harvard Review*: "Near Silk Farm Road." *Interim*: "Untitled." *Iowa Journal of Cultural Studies*: "Ode" (no. 1). *Jacket*: "Mandrakes," "Remedy." *Mike & Dale's Younger Poets*: "The Epithet *Epic*." *Proliferation*: "Ardor." *Slope*: "Poem." *The Transcendental Friend*: "Dulcinea." *Verse*: "Last in the Haughty Branch," "Sympathy and Envy," "One Day," "In What Order May I Say These Things." *Volt*: "Not Only Because We Were Wrong."

　　"A Dream of Mimesis" also appears in *Body Electric: America's Best Poetry from the* American Poetry Review (W.W. Norton, 2000). "In Las Vegas" also appears in *New Voices: University and College Poetry Prizes, Eighth Edition, 1989-1998*, edited by Heather McHugh (Academy of American Poets, forthcoming). Thanks to Charles Wright for awarding the original prize. Some of these poems appear in a chapbook entitled *Faith* (Idiom Press).

　　"Ode" (no. 1) is for Lyn Hejinian.

　　"An Interrupted Question," "Dulcinea," and "A Dream of Mimesis" were written in response to and using language from the Trask translation of Erich Auerbach's *Mimesis: The Representation of Reality in Western Literature*.

　　Thanks to John Yau's class at the Maryland Institute College of Art for producing a beautiful broadside of "Not Only Because We Were Wrong." Thanks also to the John Schlesinger fellowship program at St. Paul's School and to the Corporation of Yaddo for providing sustenance and accommodation during the preparation of this book.

　　Gratitude to the many friends and teachers who helped me in the preparation of the manuscript.

CONTENTS

I.

NOT ONLY BECAUSE WE WERE WRONG

Not only because we were wrong,
But also because we were deeply unimpressed,
Lovers were left at dusk to contemplate being alone.
Responding to being alone an intruder.
Grown to be one and not one.
As if mother had told me so.
Mother, O tell us again that we are one.
An image of a vision of——. Lately one of the ideas
I have had has been scripted out for me
And one has been wholly original and thus
Contributes to this loneliness.
One tree is lesser known object than two trees.
Two trees are more known for progeny
Glisten, gee. It is gorgeous to speak of trees.
There is no annoyance in the world.
All of us sympathize around a tree.

FALSE LIFE

Except that we had remained ordinary
In the wood
by the window
watching the two
stilted figures
discuss.

What passes between them
is the last idolatry,
of one who can speak
by the one who responds.

In response the one
holding the other.

In response the one
growing weaker,
and the other
growing gracious,
as if to show
strength.

What is it to be ordinary?
In this light,
which twitches on my
throat—

To not come from one place
but go to another.

To come from a boiler-plate
hot, charged by ether.

FALSE LIGHT

About this time, we tried our house.
We tapped at the pane and were decorous
in that on our horsebacks
we dressed in darkest suit.

In delight and fervor over there,
in the bushel and the banditry
in mountainous air and a visionary
candor.

All honesty, anatomy,
And in our hair was pearlescent
intention.

Above it all, in the window
we saw light.

AROUND A WHITE ORCHARD, A FRAME

Around a white orchard, a frame. It is winter
and the mountains hum. The birds fly,
less often now.
I see her hand, and in it dread.
Of me?
In the countryside we look for one another.
The light will hit her
throat—
The air will come and then
the downpour—. Cold,
and seasonal. In the orchard a figure
of a small painted woman.
Her hand is black with coal.

IN WHAT ORDER MAY I SAY THESE THINGS

In what order may I say these things
A light wind is blowing to the north of here
The current is swollen by rain
The engines are whirring

How should one describe these things
The wresting of knowledge from a tree
The belief in restitution when the none-of-me
Is a bathing glistening skein

We have remained here, comparatively
Eager to alight
In the house we find the restive soul that guides us
Through a conspicuous longing

How can we unwind ourselves into great garish stores of
Illimitable thought? We fathom
The water in shallow ships. We fathom
Our innards as souls and sense

A great depth. I have reached, now, the summit
Of a very high hill, in the hinterland, covered in snow
I have gotten my body here, up to the top, where the clouds hover

A NEW WAY TO LIVE

I am tired of forgiving like
At night. A forum for seriousness is like
An intervention. Pleased to be cast
As a serious aid like a pretty thing to the memory.
Like a belligerent thing in the memory true.

An attachment like trees is not like
A human attachment at all.
To hear a bell ring and then put a bell in it
Is like trees that hear the sun and then
Put a sun in it like thirst.

ARDOR

      I've slept but this has happened
yet—when the windows are dressed
in red, and the engines go by with the keening
of love birds—the last day before
the parade—everything colored
like the fifth seat from the top
of a runaway ferris wheel.

      I woke in
fits and starts, blustering
wind in the morning
and everything placid at night.

ACCORDING TO THE APPETITES

Let birds, let fly—
that it was good.
There was a night and then a day
and every living creature, moved,
was good.

The light was good, the air,
the man—the man became a living thing—
and there he put
the man who formed
the earth—no rain, no no.

When you touch delight, you will not die.

The door, the door, is hard to bear.

I shall be hidden (nothing sweet)
your days (your face) and now you might
and at the east, which he, was taken,
turned away, and heard, the voice:

      "I am open. I am
out. The firstlings and the seedlings."

II.

ODE

The intelligent bird is blue. The intelligent bird is half human.
That smart blue bird in that tree is like a whip.
The smart bird is true and desirable.
That is a feathered friend I'd like to have.
His feathers reflect the day's glare marvelously.
They add a blue shade to the scenery of the day.
In the fall it is beautiful—this tinge of blue reflected in the day.
The bird is full of strange habits.
It nips at its backside and squawks.
It nips and paces back and forth on its branch.
I wonder if it is my admiration.
No. It is simply the beauty of this intelligent blue bird.
This bird is desirable.
I've touched it when a child.
I've touched its scalp and wondered—this intelligent bird is so calm in the morning.
It is a pleasure to hear it sing. It is a pleasure to lavish attention on this bird.

MANDRAKES

These porticos under the soil
Keep their coolness by keeping their
Branches to seek for the hand shapes—
Their form has the name of the May root.

The forthrightness of trees—
With their wait for the movement,
Their long and plain patience for growing.
It is the Lent of Vegetation before it rains,
Trees waiting to take up their figures.

Under the soil is a captain—roots
Being the human form if they may. I trim
For to wait for the captain. Trim for to wait—
The sail shape is made in the image of our shape,
As if it were perfect and hadn't had motion.

That the stillness of the mandrake
That makes it the wood, not the soul
Making stillness. And if it were so, to be simple as thread,
Or to shriek like the nettles, the roots could then move
But they cannot.

IMMACULATION

Clean
I wish to be

O, major or whatever.
So that I
must lapse into this
disgusting tongue.

Rogue is like tongue
as is legend to bludgeon.

Like bludgeon the legend
kills us.

At night
the stars
are scattering.

A star is a point of light,
longer perceived
than aligned,
at night.

Rogue is like tongue
in that both of them
come into light as
disgusting anatomy.

I align myself
with noon-day thrust.
To be naked
or nude
To be brightly lit
in barnyard
swoon
alone.

NEAR SILK FARM ROAD

Love me like a vegetable.
Loosen my skin from its sternum,
Knead my breast-bone—
Suckle my gums from their jaw bone.
Kiss my molars
with your crow's thick tongue.

Touch me this morning.
Husk me like bumpy corn
shod in cob—
Leave me
to the dung beetles
and the day-long staccato of grasshopper thighs.

MY LIFE

To make an emphatic claim on
life.

It is broken and so it
experiences itself.

I recounted my development
and rather called it art
than called it
solitude.

I became a creature of night.
Moved from habitation to habitation
as if winged.

Moved and sang of a glacial sensation
Slow and superior to life.

PURSUANT

We went out to look at the sky,
at the never-changing roof-tops which I cannot see—

Looking for news of us, a red
and blue pencil gave me courage.
Of importance to me in particular, the name
of one person capable of giving me those unaccountable
hands and that voice—"knock at my door."

I recall there was almost no one—it
was a plain dirt way. "Bear to the left"
down some stone steps—that this would be
impossible—that a man might be the enemy
of other men, in the rose-glassed jar
was a "watching me."

MY LOT

Unsure of my future and lacking
consolation, I ran. The commitment

action drove me. In the winter, when the air
is clean, the meaning of oddments,

like wind, is expecting me. I am happy
with my lot. It is small, perfect, square.

It is minimal. In the morning, if the wind
is clean, I go to it. It is lovely. It moves me

from one place to another. In the midst
of the summer hills, I am lost. In the midst

of the great reprisals, of love, dearness,
chastity—lost. My lot in life.

'Twas my only companion.

ODE

I wait—
>> For its name—and
>>>> Look
How the tree—comes to
>>>> Sing to it—wait—
>>>>>> Then harass it.
I make myself like this—
>>>> And
Ask—for
The tree—
Is the weight of
The tree—and
>>>> Awaiting—my certainly musical form—
>>>>>> It will quiver—and
>>>>>>>> As it was—naked—and
This—
>>>> The idea—of the tree.

>>>>>> Yes,
>>>>>> To thee—my one beech—
>>>>>> My happy done birch tree—
>>>>>> You are so—I want it—
>>>>>> I come—hang my belt—
>>>>>> From the

Move me—
>>>> The all
>>> Me—

The sun comes

        And midday—is

                Felt about your tufted shade—

            You hear

            That I hear

            The barest of leaves—

And the beech tree—

      The birch tree—

      The tree—

      It will have me.

III.

AN INTERRUPTED QUESTION

On their way to be transported there is a question and a gust of wind.
The subject matter is love. It is characteristically true and desirable that the woman be
   young.
It is characteristically virtue that stands in the way of the matter of love.

There is, perhaps, a disorder; the woman—her face—is disordered.

There is the absorption in her.

Then the noise of the several men mounting the stairs.

There is the absorption in her and the answer: the several men mounting the stairs.

There is the disorder of her negligee, the order of the several men.

The men are coming up the stairs. As characters they inspire both pity and fear.
As figures they master the style and intent of the story and are somber.

The men who have mounted the stairs are now gruesome.
The men who have mounted the stairs are pictorial and sensory even as the boy and
   the girl remain sensual and cruel.

Gravitas itself is by no means lost—though repressed by the episode's brevity.
Its language is lost to the gory and spectral description of love.

DULCINEA

There is a permissible order to the world.
As part of it a bird will seek its prey.
As part of it a bird will spend the best part of the day at rest—
The romance in that dalliance—and this
Treatment
As it is permitted in presentation and style.
The bird is the result of an expression of desire
And of refinement.

o

                        The configuration of it as a he or as
                                a she
            is immaterial to the single vision of the two figures …
                    Of the figures as we put them
                        in a story or relationship
                    like the one between an aesthetic
            intention and the story that unfolds
                    in its place. Or the one between
                        a man and his wife
                                or an office and
                        a chief.

o

Again the Dulcinea inexhaustible and worthy.
Like the mountains—like the figure
of a bird
or of a mountain.

IN LAS VEGAS

1.

When I write a novel in Vegas, I ask myself what other people will think.

When I write a novel, I think a lot about eating.

When I call my friend, he gets very excited.

Out of my window I see a huge mountain.

Its striations make it look as if the rain has fallen sideways on it. Over the years

I have danced a lot. I have thought to become a novelist.

I see a mountain that looks as if drenched by the rain. I see a sky

Wherein clouds drift by slowly and unendingly.

Pistons go up and down. Pendulums swing back and forth.

If a person who is in love with me reads this, they will care.

If someone who hates me reads it, they will dismiss me as an impostor.

2.

Trees are like cairns. The yard is clean. The door is opened

to let in air. I have driven great distances and listened to a lot of music.

I read things that make me jealous. Alone.

I read about people I know. All women want to be beautiful.

3.

The pool's light like moonlight.

The idea is to exercise caution and not give it up to them.

To say love and not be determined to show it then makes one a bastard.

To make proclamations as these are very pretty things to make

and to script them out and cause ugly havoc in the universe

we then must know. Over the hills there are lights.

Over the hills there are lights and this heat.

You have been the measure of all greatness.

It is pleasant of you in my mind to have been so.
You please god to love then if measuring greatness within me
found succubus to be fled, sent out, and adored.
Pray for me, I be less wholesome when trees sway.
Winds. Winds go these everywhich way.

4.
I like the sky. And I do not do
the opposite of what the trees do.
Interesting. I love you
is like sitting on a bench and you don't
mean it when you say it.
Someone else has made you say it.

IN BROOKLYN

I would engage in an argument with him
then go near to dedication of a poem to him.
Bring me with you then go again I ask, fright,
Listen to me. Listen lovers
in movies who never made it
to the top of the Empire State Building, and that lovers
who never established an intimacy could make a female poet
and not a male poet though I do grow body parts
things gone then meadows

o

This is out of control enter
magical goat-herder over yon river
comes little boy/mommy. Gosh this
is it, the place known, bucolic
longing and for nothing. For little men
not up in spaceships but here in my bedroom at night and
is no one awake for me—no one to save me and
green/pink bright lustiness flung out at stars
falls to speakers who crow (mercy mercy)

o

Energetic half a mortal lifetime allowed. Command
for the truth is that skies as done masturbate lubed up 'gan sloshing—
O arthritis in the stars signals messengers to flee flee
and no rhythms to it, nothing to it but quick snaps and wings
on feet. Strange in bed. Talked of a lot and beaten into their heads
that there is a deformity. It brings out my sympathy.
It is sad.

o

Generally thinking of lines (guilt) conventional
passengers everyone was on the subway today and I
thought of an essay on sin, on the seven deadly sins
and how one could never once do or be anything but this—
and eternity faced it this generally thinking of lines (guilt)
and passing the time not well not
doing much or not working hard either gist
pay attention and I will do lots to get you to
look at me and to think of me, talk of me.

THE EMOTION AND PLEASURE OF THOUGHT

The woman
The woman is true.

That the style of her love
as it palliates
the masses—

That the style of her love
is depicted as pleasure
when truly
its style is itself
in the fashion of
pain—

The woman is surely
metaphoric and grotesque

The woman is
against us

Her hand is
draped
cruelly

Her mouth is closed gently

Her hand, now insuperable,
calls to us

We find
prurience
and justice
in every

delectation—her hand is
draped cruelly
Her mouth is closed gently
Her eyes face us

Now
they are
facing us.

We think it a painting,
this setting in which she lies

draped—

Or a theatre—

Some place of depiction.

We are aware of
how truly removed
we must be
from her life—

and renouncing
our mediocrity
we thrust ourselves
into her eyes.

A DREAM OF MIMESIS

It is duty and not hospitality that has diverted the ancient guest.

It is the whispered threat of sentiment and ignorance.

There is a plenitude of foresight. Before the diversion of the light.

The light is now spilling over. We now recognize him by his scar.

The feelings are being externalized. No contour is blurred, but of light

There is only the thin throat of it that hits his head. He rises—

Is seen through the curtains. Now lax—with the wind, made more solid. They are lying

Open. Their mouths are opening and closing, glistening

Slick in the yellow light. He is wanting to fuck.

The thigh is clean. The scar on the thigh is newly healed.

In the episode's chaste entrée ("once … when a boar …")—here—

He must straddle her ass. We are patient. Here, his organs begin to swell—

Lest they are spiritual, his courage will fail him. His organs are swelling—we have, here,

Great depths—trimmed by delicate vulvic folds. Flesh dangles, cut.

They talk. Her hand, fraught, grabs at his clean, polished cock.

Gradually, historically, the choice has befallen him. Idols aged rot on the verge

Of legend. It runs too smoothly. The river beside her. Angst. The river is blue.

The river is not very wide. He is raping her. The situation is complicated.

The scar on his thigh is newly healed. Let's not see it just yet—let's see

Both of their bodies illuminated in a uniform fashion. He slaps her. She grabs

At his ass. A suggestive influence of the unexpressed. The separation of styles.

Light hits her throat. The thighs of each swell—then abate. The sublime action dulls
    them.

He "persecutes" her. He is not afraid to let the realism of daily life enter into his sublime.

There are clearly expressible reasons for their conflict. The human problem has dealt
    with them

In this fashion. They are using two styles. The concept of his historical becoming has
    disturbed him
Into action. The episodic nature of her pain is obscured by the sublime action of his cock.
He is the simile of the wolf. He is seeking her nipples with his mouth ("A god himself
Gave him …"). The introduction of episodes. An eloquent foreground. A uniform present
Entirely foreign to the story of his scar ("The woman now touched it …")

THE EPITHET *EPIC*

1.

Their thoughts are entirely immersed in resolution.

He resolves to consecrate it with a tree.

He opens his eyes and he finds a place fitting to planting.

It is early in the morning. When he comes he is ethical.

He will remember it. He will give it the epithet *epic* and leave it.

Where is he?

In the country there are two of them.

Standing immersed in the shadow of love.

Of his motives, he says they are pure.

Of the heavy silence, she thinks it is part of the trueness of their love.

In the winter his motives are altered by a storm.

The two of them purchase a knife.

The blade of it is long and thin.

He commands her to speak in direct discourse.

He indicates that he wants her to express her thoughts concisely and with precision.

He finds this romantic.

They are in the country and her bodice has been cut with the knife.

Part of it hangs off her shoulder. In the distance she hears the sound of a gunshot.

Their speech no longer serves them adequately.

2.

He walks toward her, feels her breast.

He places his lips on hers. Pulls her down. Puts his hand far up her skirt and she sighs
    for him.

Their skin is taut, bumpy.

He is no longer in a predicament.

She tilts her head back and moans. She lilts her voice slightly and asks him if he loves
her.

He does love her. He feels a very true love for her.

He is then quite unable to continue. He is breathing too heavily and doesn't want to be
speaking anymore.

She is also breathing heavily.

They come. They are happy.

IV.

ONE DAY

Having scoured his temperament's face long and loud,
Dead and door-well
He laid me through beheaded morning
Into beaded day.

One day, while leaning against a pole and as one may say that
The pole was sweet—once
It had taupe on it, clear and strange
And did gleam like light—

Like you, love, or bosom,
You heave and are majestical. So when
Lost in stem or straw,
Brain-wise at least if not
Bodily thawed
In conjugation's lisp.

Alas it is likely an awful laboratory in which I concoct you
Therefore shall I keep the flame and the sick of heart interior as if,
Through a window, one could see your open grave.
The flowing scene and spirit within
The pearl in the solemn stream
And broken brook, I can hear it move haggard over rocks
Advancing, slow, along the path
To its settlement
And footstep,
Where it may or may not
Remain
Resembling, along, like a brook
Dry, parched, and of no substance.

I THINK IT'S MY FATE

Of who we should be I make one more recommendation—
Still sitting I make an unlimited final instruction
To you—who all know, who have all heard the
Stories that make one to think that
Still lurking within every happenstance
Heated reaction are schedules
Of what's there to be though
The new air is heating our brisk promenades and
The old air is carefully keeping our
Mental acuity down to a minimum
Only at night when it's late and we've
Got to talk. Tide is to lightning
What's happening isn't there something?

SYMPATHY AND ENVY

Until my friends abducted me
The world was a cubicle
The point where the passage runs east to west puzzles me
Your world
It is you and, it seems, through you
I see myself
To the south is a portent
An asking for work and a shower
A cubicle
Benched
Over the horizon is the greatest writer ever to have lived
He is not blind nor sure
He is nothing and has never written anything
We care about
As we do about ourselves
If we write
As the world will go
We'll go
And we will
Pretend
In the presence
Of delinquency and parody
There are animals bursting and lacerated
By the strokes of bells
There are lashings of the soul, a trill
The movements of assassins and hunger
The world is formidable and proud
It is angry.

The four points of laughter recede into heaven
We stand and listen
We know them we
Know ourselves
This advance should not now be the last
In our last breath the gleaming reminiscent teeth the scrotum
And disgust—it was rotund
It was extemporaneously pleasant
It was legal and menial
Our shoulders will leave us
Our voices will bleat
Help us the world is lost
Help us
We get what we want.

LAST IN THE HAUGHTY BRANCH

Last in the haughty branch, over the bird's head and into the mouth of the turtle dove
Whistling
To the wind
Of conformity
Equality
The popularity of the wicket and the fence
And of the seedling, within it a great potentiality
An abrogation of the glorious, an arrogance of beauty
The forthright tree in front of me
The gloomy dark
Botanical
The barking dog
The pleasing whistle of the house on fire
The gorgeous appraisal of the muscle of the heart
When no longer in love.
Over the conceit and the attraction of the crooked court
The bankers who vaunt it
And the rapid reversal of fortune—.
The world goes to hell
In the envelope, we listen
For the great words of dejection and of blasphemy,
The wind makes plain.

REMEDY

When the trees gave off
     a pittance
The blooms
       no good to eat—

Put shit in a jar
        Restore it—
the barren Will
     Find its remedy in the half-contained
        jewel box
     With four of your fingers
         the jar to your mouth—

Hot water and rose petals
          adjudicating—
   you will have to own up
     to this. The water
       as a stand in for,
     and the petals as symbols of,
        the two slim lips—

Then, with your bile at a stand-still
     and your face at a stand-still
Go find a woman
   and drain your semen into her

The madrigal song
　　　　of renewal
will lease out your heart to your body—
　　　and your soul will
　　　　　　　　solicit your soul

SICK AND SIN

My purse is made of sick and sin
Of penitence, a pansy—

      I would be cleft—

The ballot is brief, the purse is in tone
as a ballot and is itself defined by its habit
as a purse.

The silver sorrow is as an arrow
and tomorrow my purse is as
sick and as sin—

      I would prick it

Would send silver arrows to prickle me
post-chance and as does befit a purse

A mouth borrowed
for the purpose of pursing—

      A borrowed bath—

THE WAGES OF SIN

Grief and it fleeth—
Streets and it tributes
to nature
to think on it—

Certainly
it is a heaven upon earth—
to imagine it certainly
death is due
nature—

That parts the most vital—
The quickest of sense is
that sometimes

We see error, in the light
upon the vantage rest.

POEM

I think of your face and of its deepest bewilderment.
       It makes me sad as if the morning
were a tower or pair
       of them—haunted and pure,
degenerate, elevated, strange of view
       in solitude.

UNTITLED

It was the answer to a question.
As if a sensation, derailed, had found place
      in something it could never be.
The threat of finding place in what one
      cannot be.
I have expected you, who now arrive, and I can see your form
      in the doorway, and I ask you what we
      cannot be.
Light is conducting us in toward a unity, but our instinct is against it.
If we, who are answers to questions, come to this,
      this inclusiveness
      will ruin us—.
Lodged in strict formation,
      we are diffuse,
and so we wonder
      what we are.

ABOUT THE AUTHOR

Originally from New Hampshire, Katy Lederer was educated at the University of California, Berkeley, and the Iowa Writers' Workshop, where she was an Iowa Arts Fellow. Her poems have appeared in *Jacket, Fence, Harvard Review, The Verse Book of New American Poets* and *Body Electric: America's Best Poetry from the* American Poetry Review, among other publications. Since 1996, she has edited her own magazine, *Explosive*, as well as a series of limited-edition chapbooks under the imprint Spectacular Books. She lives in New York City.

ABOUT THE BOOK

Cover design by Jeff Clark.
Book design by Brian Henry.
Set in Bell.
Printed by Thomson-Shore on acid-free, recycled paper.